D0064383

A Marshall Edition
Edited and designed by Marshall Editions
The Orangery
161 New Bond Street
London W1Y 9PA

Original concept by Mike Foster

First published in the U.S.A. by Scholastic Inc.
555 Broadway, New York, NY 10012
SCHOLASTIC and associated logos are trademarks and/or
registered trademarks of Scholastic Inc.

10 9 8 7 6 5 4 3 2 1   8 9/9 0/0 01 02 03

Library of Congress Cataloging-in-Publishing data available.

ISBN 0-590-11920-6

Consultant, United States:
Dr. Carol A. Benson
Andrew W. Mellon Fellow, Ancient Art
The Walters Art Gallery
Baltimore, Maryland.

Consultant, United Kingdom:
Felicity Cobbing
Palestine Exploration Fund, London.
Formerly of the British Museum,
Department of Western Asiatic Antiquities.

Printed and bound in Portugal
by Printer Portugesa.
Originated in the UK
by Jade Reprographics.

First Scholastic printing,
November 1998

The Traveler's Guide to
ANCIENT
GREECE

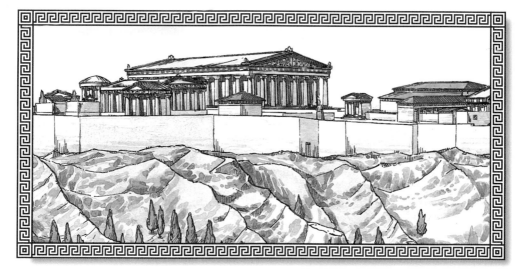

Written by FIONA MACDONALD
Illustrated by MIKE FOSTER

Scholastic Inc.
New York • Toronto • London • Auckland • Sydney

UNDERSTANDING DATES

Many historians use a calendar that divides the past into two separate eras: B.C. (before Jesus Christ) and A.D. (Latin initials that mean "The Year of our Lord"). They call the year that Jesus Christ was born "1 A.D." They count forward from year 1 in the A.D. era, and backward from year 1 in the B.C. era.

SPELLING GREEK WORDS

The ancient Greeks used a different alphabet from the one used in many parts of the world today. Scholars have invented different ways of translating these ancient Greek letters into modern non-Greek spellings. This means that you may find the spelling of some ancient Greek words vary, especially peoples' names and place names. In this book the spellings are based on Roman translations, because today's alphabet is a modern version of the Roman alphabet.

KEY TO ABBREVIATIONS

km = kilometer/
    kilometre
m = meter/metre
ft = foot
cm = centimeter/
    centimetre
g = gram/gramme
lb = pound
oz = ounce
kg = kilogram/
    kilogramme
l = liter/litre

CONTENTS

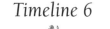
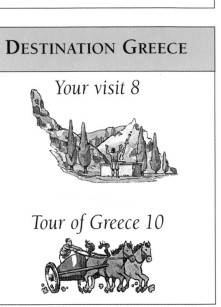

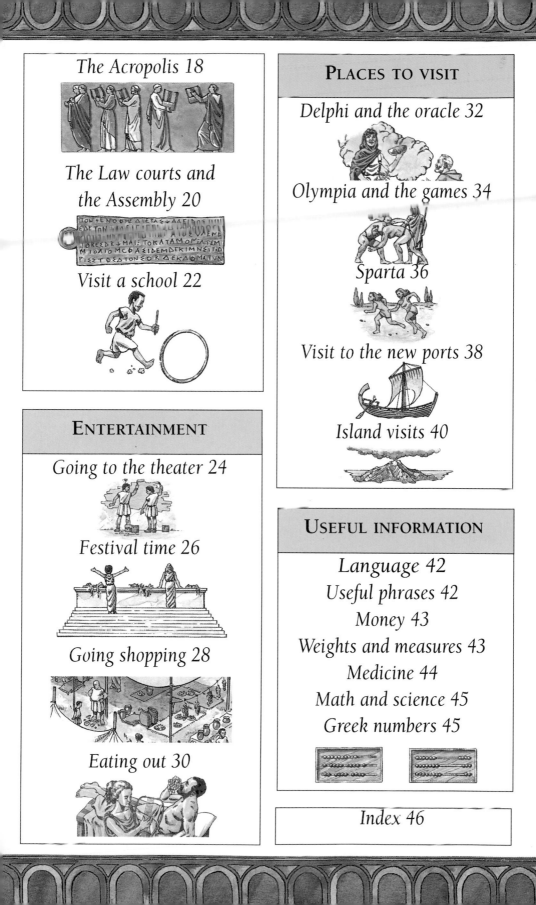

Welcome! This book will be your guide as you visit ancient Greece. It will help you explore Greece's wild and beautiful landscape, wander around its crowded cities, and witness some of its world famous events. Among many other things, this guide will show you how to buy pottery from a potter's workshop and what to expect from a trip to a Greek theater. This book looks at Greece toward the end of the fifth century B.C., when Greek civilization was at its height.

Mask found at Mycenae

As you can see from the timeline opposite, the Greeks have had a long and eventful history. The earliest inhabitants of Greece lived first as hunters, then as farmers. By 3,000 B.C., they had been conquered by the Minoan dynasty of kings who lived on the island of Crete. Then, around 2,100 B.C., the first Greek-speaking settlers arrived, from lands to the north and east, and a new "Greek" civilization began.

This civilization lasted almost 2,000 years until Greece was conquered by Roman armies in 146 B.C. But even then, it did not completely disappear. Today, people in many parts of the world still use ancient Greek words, think about Greek ideas, and admire ancient Greek works of art.

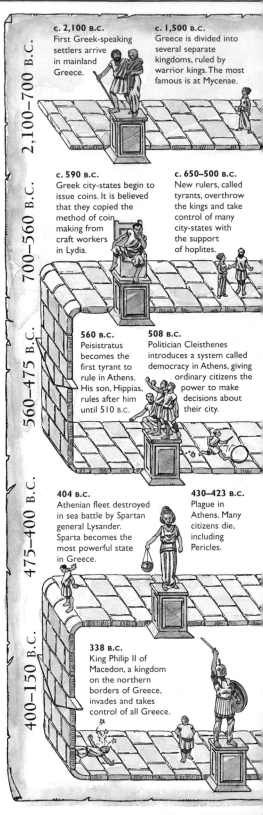

2,100–700 B.C.

c. 2,100 B.C.
First Greek-speaking settlers arrive in mainland Greece.

c. 1,500 B.C.
Greece is divided into several separate kingdoms, ruled by warrior kings. The most famous is at Mycenae.

700–560 B.C.

c. 590 B.C.
Greek city-states begin to issue coins. It is believed that they copied the method of coin making from craft workers in Lydia.

c. 650–500 B.C.
New rulers, called tyrants, overthrow the kings and take control of many city-states with the support of hoplites.

560–475 B.C.

560 B.C.
Peisistratus becomes the first tyrant to rule in Athens. His son, Hippias, rules after him until 510 B.C.

508 B.C.
Politician Cleisthenes introduces a system called democracy in Athens, giving ordinary citizens the power to make decisions about their city.

475–400 B.C.

404 B.C.
Athenian fleet destroyed in sea battle by Spartan general Lysander. Sparta becomes the most powerful state in Greece.

430–423 B.C.
Plague in Athens. Many citizens die, including Pericles.

400–150 B.C.

338 B.C.
King Philip II of Macedon, a kingdom on the northern borders of Greece, invades and takes control of all Greece.

c. 1,100–1,050 B.C.
Greek Iron Age begins. Greek craft workers discover how to smelt iron and shape it into weapons and tools.

c. 800–700 B.C.
Greece divides into small city-states, each with its own government.

c. 800–700 B.C.
The poet Homer creates two epic poems—the *Iliad* and the *Odyssey*—by collecting and writing down fragments of earlier poems.

c. 700 B.C.
A new way of fighting is introduced by city-states—using citizen armies of foot soldiers, called "hoplites."

c. 777–500 B.C.
Greek city-states establish colonies along the shores of the Mediterranean Sea and the Black Sea.

776 B.C.
Traditional date of the first Olympic games. However, games may have been held, unrecorded, at least 500 years before.

499–490 B.C.
The Persians attack Greece. After nine years of fighting, the Persians are defeated at the Battle of Marathon.

482 B.C.
Athens builds a new fleet to protect Greece from further invasion.

480–479 B.C.
The Persians invade Greece again. They are defeated in two battles—Salamis (at sea) and Plataea (fought on land with hoplites).

447 B.C.
Building work begins on the Parthenon, the great temple to the Goddess Athena, on the Acropolis in Athens.

461 B.C.
Athenian politician and war-leader Pericles wins the support of citizens in the Assembly at Athens.

461 B.C.
Sparta attacks Athens. This marks the start of a series of battles known as the Peloponnesian War.

336 B.C.
King Philip is murdered, and his son, Alexander the Great, seizes power.

334–326 B.C.
Alexander leads his army out of Greece and conquers the mighty Persian Empire.

323 B.C.
Alexander the Great dies, and his empire, including Greece, is divided among his generals.

146 B.C.
Greece is invaded and conquered by a new power in the Mediterranean World—the Roman Empire.

Note
The c. before a date, such as c. 1,000 B.C., is an abbreviation for *circa*, the Latin word for "about" or "around."

YOUR VISIT

You've chosen to visit Greece at a good time! In the 5th century B.C., Greece is at the height of its power. You will find that Greek city-states are rich and strong. Only recently, their soldiers and sailors fought off invaders from neighboring lands. You will also discover that Greek people are great artists and craft workers. Their cities are full of beautiful temples and lifelike statues made from marble and bronze. The Greeks are great scholars, scientists, and thinkers, and they love to talk! You can look forward to many interesting discussions.

The Ancient Greek World
This map shows ancient Greece and its surrounding colonies (light pink areas) in the late 5th century B.C. Since 775 B.C. Greek civilization has expanded greatly, and Greek people inhabit not only the Greek mainland and the surrounding islands, but also can be found in places as far as the Black Sea and North Africa.

• Rome

ADRIATIC
SEA

ITALY

SICILY

IONIAN
SEA

Carthage •

Greek homelands

Greek colonies

City-states
Greece is divided into many small city-states. Each contains a city and all the land nearby, and has its own army and laws. City-states are to be found all over Greece, within various regions. For example, Sparta is a city-state in the Peloponnese region (see pages 10–11).

POPULATION
c. 450 B.C.

Athens (city) 170,000

Attica (city-state) 350,000

Sparta (city-state) 25,000

**Greek mainland
and islands** 2,000,000

Carthage (city-state) 700,000

N

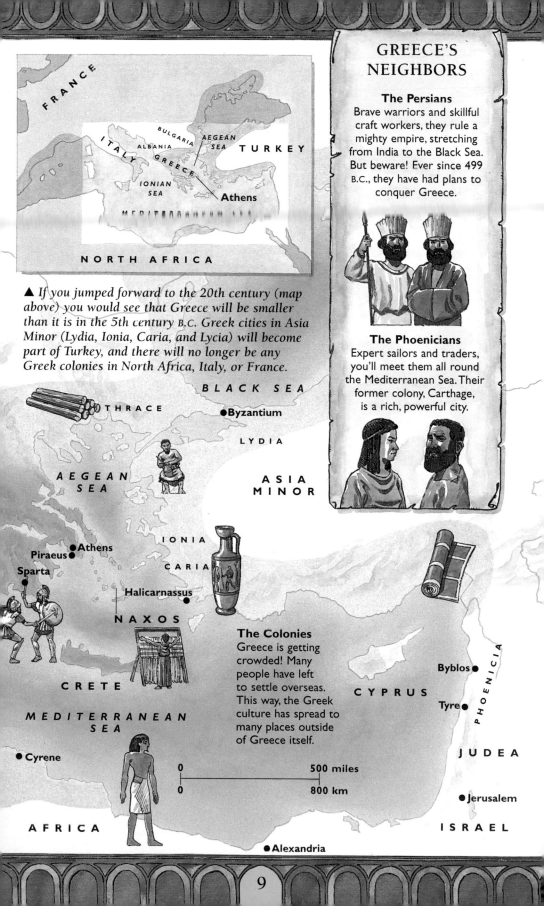

GREECE'S NEIGHBORS

The Persians
Brave warriors and skillful craft workers, they rule a mighty empire, stretching from India to the Black Sea. But beware! Ever since 499 B.C., they have had plans to conquer Greece.

The Phoenicians
Expert sailors and traders, you'll meet them all round the Mediterranean Sea. Their former colony, Carthage, is a rich, powerful city.

▲ *If you jumped forward to the 20th century (map above) you would see that Greece will be smaller than it is in the 5th century B.C. Greek cities in Asia Minor (Lydia, Ionia, Caria, and Lycia) will become part of Turkey, and there will no longer be any Greek colonies in North Africa, Italy, or France.*

The Colonies
Greece is getting crowded! Many people have left to settle overseas. This way, the Greek culture has spread to many places outside of Greece itself.

Map labels:

FRANCE · ITALY · BULGARIA · ALBANIA · GREECE · AEGEAN SEA · TURKEY · IONIAN SEA · Athens · MEDITERRANEAN SEA · NORTH AFRICA

BLACK SEA · THRACE · Byzantium · LYDIA · AEGEAN SEA · ASIA MINOR · IONIA · Athens · Piraeus · CARIA · Sparta · Halicarnassus · NAXOS · CRETE · MEDITERRANEAN SEA · Cyrene · AFRICA · CYPRUS · Byblos · Tyre · PHOENICIA · JUDEA · Jerusalem · ISRAEL · Alexandria

0 — 500 miles
0 — 800 km

By foot

This is the way to meet people! Most Greeks travel on foot.

Mule or horse

If you travel on foot, take a mule or packhorse to carry your bags.

In a chariot

If you have the money, hire a horse-drawn chariot with a charioteer. But it can only travel safely over flat land.

By ship

This is the easiest way to reach many places in Greece. However, watch out for pirates and sudden storms.

KEY TO MAP

CITY-STATES

RELIGIOUS SITES

BATTLE SITES

TOUR OF GREECE

The Greeks are very proud of their beautiful homeland. So don't feel shy about praising all the wonderful sights you will see as you travel around. Greece is a wild, rugged country, with high, snow-capped mountains, steep valleys, and rough stony soil. There are hundreds of rocky islands all around the coast. The hills are covered with thick forests of oak and fir trees, and on the mountain pastures, you can find many wildflowers and sweet-smelling herbs. There is very little flat land or fertile soil; the best farmland is in Macedonia, Thessaly, and Thrace.

Dodona
Visit the Holy Oak at this ancient shrine, sacred to Zeus. People say the rustlings of its leaves are the words of Zeus himself.

MACEDONIA

Mount Olympus

E P I R U S

Dodona

T H E S S A L Y

G R E E C E

MOUNT OLYMPUS p 33

I O N I A N SEA

Delphi

P E L O P O N N E S E

Olympia

THE SANCTUARY AT DELPHI pp 32–33

Sparta

Things to remember on your journey
Greek weather can be unpredictable, so take a warm cloak and a hat to protect yourself from sudden storms; take strong, comfortable walking shoes (Greek sandals have thick cork soles). Greece is an earthquake zone, so ask Poseidon, the "earth-shaker" god, to protect you, by making an offering at his shrine.

The Peloponnese
Go carefully here! In recent years, this has become a war zone. Athens has been fighting against Sparta.

▶ *You must buy something to take home to remind you of your visit. We recommend a beautiful vase—Greek potters make the best in the world!*

T H R A C E

A E G E A N   S E A

Lesbos

LESBOS (and other islands) pp 40–41

Marathon
For many Greeks, this is holy ground. A famous battle was fought here against the Persians in 490 B.C. The Greeks won, but many brave soldiers died.

Thebes

Marathon

A T T I C A

• Corinth

Athens

ATHENS pp 12–31

SPARTA pp 36–37

CLIMATE AND LANDSCAPE

Highest Mountains
Mount Olympus
9,570 ft (2,917 m)
Mount Pindus 7,497 ft
(2,285 m)

Area (mainland Greece)
31,504 sq. miles (81,590 km²)

Coastline (mainland Greece)
About 2,486 miles (4,000 km)

Temperature (Athens)
July average 80°F (26°C)
January average 49°F (9.4°C)
In the mountains and the north, it can be much colder, with snow in summertime!

Rain and Sun
Athens: annual average
16 in. (40.6 cm)
Mount Olympus: annual average 47 in. (119 cm)
Days of sunshine: average 300 per year

When to visit
Spring: warm and showery.
Summer: very hot and dry.
Can be windy.
Fall: warm. Torrential rains.
Winter: cold and damp.

JOURNEY PLANNER

Delphi
Approximately 230 miles (370 km) from Athens. Take the coast road and travel as far as you can by chariot.

Olympia
Approximately 345 miles (555 km) from Athens overland, 630 miles (1,014 km) by sea.

Sparta
Approximately 305 miles (490 km) from Athens. A long trek through wild, hilly countryside.

Lesbos
Approximately 480 miles (772 km) from Athens. Travel by ship, via Piraeus.

WHERE TO STAY

Greek people are very friendly and hospitable. It is an honor for them to welcome guests into their homes. Many citizens will be happy to rent you a room. So it should not be difficult to find a place to stay!

The standard of housing varies throughout the city. A few very rich families live in splendid two-story homes. They might have running water from a diverted stream and an earth-pit lavatory. But most homes are not like this. Craftsmen and merchants live in fairly comfortable houses, often built in blocks. Poor people live in simple shacks or rent a room in a larger home.

Busy port
You will arrive at Piraeus, a busy harbor about seven miles (11.3 km) from Athens. It is an important fishing port and shipbuilding center.

Hotel accommodations
Many big towns in Greece offer luxury hotel accommodations. Poorer travelers to Greece often sleep in doorways of public buildings or porches.

The port of Piraeus has recently been rebuilt to the designs drawn up by town planner Hippodamus of Miletus. Streets, houses, and shops are laid out neatly in a grid design.

Foreigners
Athens is home to many people from other places. They do all sorts of jobs but unlike the citizens, they cannot take part in political life and have fewer civil rights.

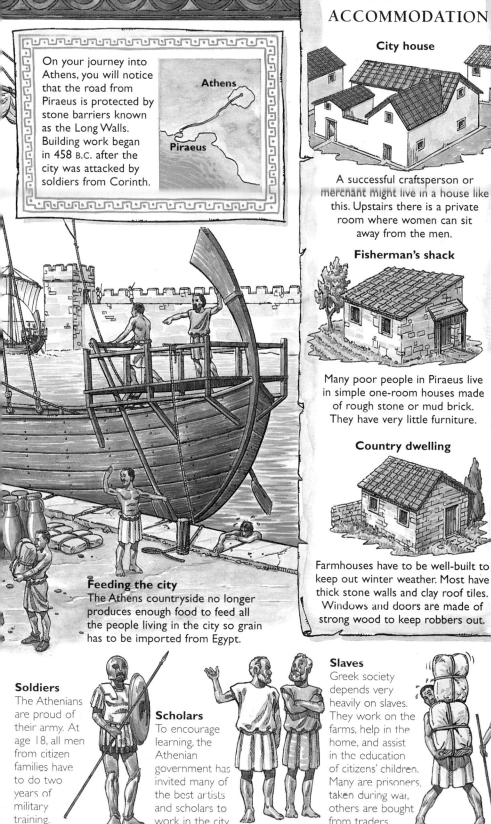

On your journey into Athens, you will notice that the road from Piraeus is protected by stone barriers known as the Long Walls. Building work began in 458 B.C. after the city was attacked by soldiers from Corinth.

Athens

Piraeus

ACCOMMODATION

City house

A successful craftsperson or merchant might live in a house like this. Upstairs there is a private room where women can sit away from the men.

Fisherman's shack

Many poor people in Piraeus live in simple one-room houses made of rough stone or mud brick. They have very little furniture.

Country dwelling

Farmhouses have to be well-built to keep out winter weather. Most have thick stone walls and clay roof tiles. Windows and doors are made of strong wood to keep robbers out.

Feeding the city
The Athens countryside no longer produces enough food to feed all the people living in the city so grain has to be imported from Egypt.

Soldiers
The Athenians are proud of their army. At age 18, all men from citizen families have to do two years of military training.

Scholars
To encourage learning, the Athenian government has invited many of the best artists and scholars to work in the city.

Slaves
Greek society depends very heavily on slaves. They work on the farms, help in the home, and assist in the education of citizens' children. Many are prisoners, taken during war, others are bought from traders.

All women,
except slaves,
wear their hair
long. Most Greek
men have their
hair cut fairly
short, and wear
neatly trimmed
beards.

Diadems

Smartly dressed
married women
hold their hair
back with a metal
band called
a diadem.

Slaves

Busy women
slaves need a
style that is neat
and easy to care
for. Short hair is
also a sign that
they are not free.

Mature style

Older women
wear their hair
tied neatly with
a scarf.

Beards

The Greeks
admire beards.
They think they
are manly.

WHAT TO WEAR

Greek clothes are designed to be comfortable. They are easy and elegant to wear, and you will find them very cool for traveling in. Greeks take great care with their appearance and aim to look fit, healthy, youthful, and prosperous.

Greek clothing styles do not change much from year to year. Fashionable people display their up-to-date style by their choice of hairstyle and jewelry, and by the texture and color of the clothes they wear. Very fine, smooth wool and glossy, imported silk are the most fashionable fabrics. Bright colors are popular with rich women; purple is the most expensive shade. Ordinary people wear cream-colored clothes made from undyed linen or wool.

Suntans?
Greek sun is very hot, but it is unfashionable for rich women to have a tan. So they protect their skin with veils, hats, or sunshades carried by slaves.

Getting dressed
Rich men and women have slaves to help them arrange their clothing in elegant folds.

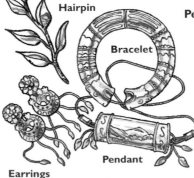

Hairpin

Bracelet

Pendant

Earrings

Peplos (short-sleeved tunic)

◀ *If you meet wealthy Greek women, you will notice their amazing jewelry. It is fashionable to wear glittering jewelry made from silver, gold, and precious stones. Favorite jewels include earrings, bracelets, necklaces, pendants, and delicate hairpins shaped like leaves and flowers.*

◀ *Greeks admire beautiful bodies, and they like to keep clean. They wash often in shallow bathtubs made of baked clay. Slaves or housewives get water from public wells. After bathing, Greeks like to rub their bodies with olive oil.*

Chiton (long-sleeved tunic)

Work clothes
Workmen and male slaves need clothes that are easy to move about in. So they wear short chitons, or a loincloth.

Cloaks
Cloaks can be draped around the body in many ways. They are made from all kinds of fabric, from silk to wool.

Chiton

Himation (cloak)

Short cloak

SHOES AND HATS

Sandals

Many Greeks go barefoot, especially indoors. When shoes are appropriate, they wear leather sandals or shoes. Follow their example if you are planning to travel far along rocky mountain paths!

Hats

Greeks wear wide-brimmed leather hats to keep dry in the rain, woven straw hats to keep cool in the summer, or fur-lined caps to keep out winter cold.

◀ *Men's and women's clothes are very similar in design—just tunics, pinned together and belted around the waist. But men's clothes are usually short, while women's clothes are always long. Old men and rich nobles sometimes wear long robes, too.*

GREEK FASHIONS

Doric peplos
A simple, sleeveless tunic worn by people in Athens and mainland Greece. It is made from a single rectangle of cloth, fastened with pins.

Ionian chiton
A long-sleeved tunic worn by people in Asia Minor and the Greek islands. It is made from two squares of fabric pinned together at the top.

Odeon

Public concerts have been held in Athens ever since 446 B.C. Pericles had this concert hall built as part of his plan to beautify the city.

Temple of Hephaestus

This massive building stands in the agora. It was built in just five years, but decorated with sculptures somewhat later (by 416 B.C.).

The Theater of Dionysus

Top Athenian dramatists write plays to be performed at this open-air theater, which is dedicated to the god of wine, dancing, and drama.

Ruins of Cyclopean Walls

These walls are the remains of a fortress built many years ago by earlier inhabitants of Athens. They are huge—16 feet (4.9 m) thick!

CITY PANORAMA

Athens is cradled among mountains on a stretch of flat land looking south to the sea. Two rocky cliffs rise up from the plain, the mountain of Lykabettos and the Acropolis Hill. Climb to the top of the Acropolis, look over the walls, and you will see the city spread out at your feet.

People come to Athens from far and wide. Politicians, merchants and traders, artists and scholars, and many tourists, like yourself, visit this magnificent city.

The Acropolis
"Acropolis" means "high city." It is the name given to this steep, rocky hill 512 ft (156 m) high. At first a fortress stood here, but now the hill is topped by many splendid temples. The rest of the city sprawls on the flat land around the bottom of the hill.

PERICLES c. 495–429 B.C.

General Pericles, Athens' most famous statesman, died recently. He was leader of the government from 443 B.C. until his death in 429 B.C. He made his name by criticizing the existing leader and demanding reforms. Pericles was a successful war leader against Sparta in 446–445 B.C. As well as strengthening Athens' control of its empire, he also insisted that the Athenian system of democracy should operate throughout the empire. But Pericles' greatest achievement was probably his plan to fill the city with wonderful new buildings and to encourage science and the arts. He aimed to make Athens "an education to Greece."

Columns

The Greeks build with three styles of column, known as orders. The simplest and most popular order is Doric. The Ionic order is more decorative. The newer Corinthian design, which is even more elaborate, has developed from the Ionic column.

Doric   **Ionic**   **Corinthian**

The Agora

The agora (marketplace) is the trading center of the city. A fine new temple, dedicated to Hephaestus, god of blacksmiths and craft workers, can be found close by.

The Panathenaic Way

This important roadway runs from the city walls to the top of the Acropolis, passing the agora on the way. It takes its name from a grand procession that marches along it during the Panathenaia, a religious festival in honor of the goddess Athena.

BUILDING A TEMPLE

The Greeks believe that temples are homes for the gods. So they design them to look like traditional Greek houses. These were originally made of wood, with tree trunks holding up a roof.

Floor

First the architects plan and measure out the foundation. Then they build a stone platform for the floor.

Columns

These are cut from blocks of stone and shaped into cylindrical sections. Beautiful white marble is quarried from the mountains near Athens.

Construction

Sections of each column are carefully shaped and fitted, then joined together with wooden pegs.

Roof

Finally, the roof is put on. Most temples have roofs made of clay tiles or thin slabs of marble.

Ilissos River
Parthenon
City walls
Acropolis
Theater of Dionysus
Pnyx
The agora
Cyclopean Walls, around the top of the Acropolis
The Panathenaic Way
The Temple of Hephaestus

◄ *The city of Athens is ringed by mountains, and the Ilissos River runs close by. The whole city is surrounded by strong walls. Only the stadium, where races are run during the Panathenaic Games, stands outside.*

Each god and goddess has their own special priests and priestesses. They lead prayers and organize sacrifices. If ceremonies are not performed correctly, the gods will be angry.

Sacrifices

Animals are sacrificed to the gods because the Greeks believe that gods, like humans, enjoy a good meal! The priests and worshipers eat the meat, leaving the fat and bones for the gods.

Offerings

People who cannot afford to sacrifice animals to the gods offer them small cakes instead. They also pour a drink of wine for the gods. Many homes have a small altar where families say prayers and make offerings every day.

THE ACROPOLIS

The Acropolis in Athens is an ancient holy site. Legends tell how, long ago, the god Poseidon and the goddess Athena quarreled over who should protect the city. Athena gave the city its first olive tree and won the favor of the people. Ever since then, the Athenians have worshiped an olive-wood statue of Athena.

After the Persians destroyed many of the buildings on the Acropolis in 480 B.C., some new temples and statues were built under the orders of the great leader Pericles. It was his ambition to make Athens the most beautiful city in Greece.

▼ *This huge statue of Athena stands inside the Parthenon. It is made of gold and ivory and is over 39 ft (11.8 m) tall. Building work was finished and the statue dedicated in 438 B.C.*

Festivals
The Panathenaia festival is held every summer to celebrate Athena's birthday. Citizens carrying offerings take part in a grand procession up to the Parthenon.

The *peplos*
The citizens also make a new robe, called a *peplos*, to present to Athena. It is so big that it has to be carried by several people.

THE ACROPOLIS

The Parthenon stands in the center of the Acropolis. Close by is the Erechtheum, a temple dedicated to Poseidon (a god) and Erechtheus (a local hero). Its roof is supported by statues of women, called caryatids. There is also an outdoor statue of Athena Promachos (Athena the Champion) made of glistening bronze. When the sun shines, the tip of Athena's spear is visible to sailors far out at sea. The little temple of Nike is dedicated to the goddess of victory. The Propylaea is a grand gateway guarding the entrance to the holy site.

Use of paint

Bright red and blue paints are often used to color the background of friezes, as seen here. Painting the friezes adds depth and life to the sculpted figures.

Proportions

Greek architects calculate the floor area, the number of columns, their height, and the distance between them to try to create a balanced design.

THE PARTHENON FRIEZE

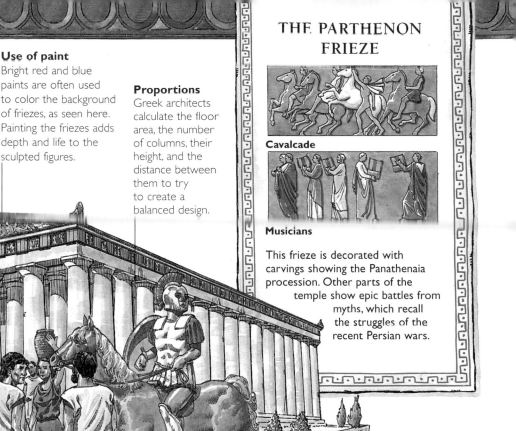

Cavalcade

Musicians

This frieze is decorated with carvings showing the Panathenaia procession. Other parts of the temple show epic battles from myths, which recall the struggles of the recent Persian wars.

◀ The Parthenon temple is one of the finest buildings in Greece. Building work started in 448 B.C. and was completed by 432 B.C. The builders used glittering white marble from nearby Mount Pentelicon, and chose the simple Doric style.

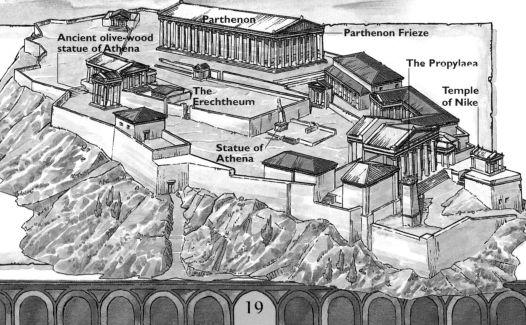

Ancient olive-wood statue of Athena

Parthenon

Parthenon Frieze

The Propylaea

The Erechtheum

Statue of Athena

Temple of Nike

Ambitious politician and army commander. Pupil of Socrates. He has just been elected as one of the generals known as *strategoi*.

Aspasia
(born c. 465 B.C.)

Pericles' companion. Beautiful and intelligent, she discussed politics with him. She is not Athenian—she was born in Miletus, on the Asia Minor coast—so many citizens distrust her.

Thucydides
(born 460 B.C.)

Historian, politician, and army commander. He is currently writing a history book on the war between Athens and Sparta.

THE LAW COURTS AND THE ASSEMBLY

Visit these sites to discover how Athenian government works. Athens is a democracy—which means it is governed by its citizens. This system of government was first introduced in Athens in 508 B.C. by a politician named Cleisthenes. Only adult men born in the city-state are counted as "citizens"—foreigners, women, and slaves have no democratic rights. All adult men have the right to attend the Assembly, where they discuss how Athens should be run, then vote on what actions to take. Citizens also serve as jurors in the law courts and elect army commanders.

▶ *The Assembly is the main decision-making body in Athens. It also appoints officials to run the city. The Assembly meets every 10 days. Groups of 50 Council members take it in turn to be on 24-hour duty to deal with emergencies.*

ATHENS' GOVERNMENT

The Assembly
approves or rejects proposals made by the Council.

The Council
is made up of 500 citizens, chosen each year by lot. It makes new policies and laws for the Assembly to discuss.

Generals
are army commanders. They also carry out laws the Assembly approves. Ten are elected by the citizens every year.

Rhetors
The ability to speak well in public is essential for any citizen who wants to play a leading part in politics. Good speakers, called *rhetors*, can persuade members of the Assembly to accept their ideas.

TOOLS OF DEMOCRACY

▼ Lists like these, showing the names of cities in the Athenian Empire and the taxes they pay, are displayed in the Acropolis.

Pnyx Hill
The Assembly meets here. At least 6,000 citizens have to attend for valid decisions to be made.

Democracy
Citizens vote at the Assembly on all the most important issues affecting city life.

Ballot disks
Each juror in the law courts is given a disk for "guilty" and one for "not guilty." The verdict is made by handing one of them in.

Ostraca
If citizens want to get rid of a politician, they write his name on a piece of broken pot. If there are over 6,000 pieces he has to leave Athens for 10 years.

Water clock
This times the length of each speech in the law courts. When all the water has trickled out of the upper pot the speaker has to stop.

THE ATHENIAN EMPIRE

In 478 B.C., many city-states formed a league for defense. As the richest and strongest, Athens soon took political control. The pink areas on the map show the Athenian Empire.

THE JUSTICE SYSTEM IN ATHENS

Selecting a jury
Any citizen can volunteer for jury service by turning up at court. Officials use a machine called a *cleroteria*, which, using colored pebbles, operates like a lottery to randomly select jurors.

Who can speak?
Only citizens can speak in the law courts. There are no lawyers, but citizens can hire speech writers to help them.

Punishment
Convicted criminals are fined, banished, or sent to work in the silver mines. This is a terrible punishment, since many mine workers die.

Knucklebones

These are tiny ankle bones from sheep and goats. Children toss them in the air, using the back of their hand, and try to catch them before they touch the ground.

Spinning tops

Children whip the tops with a leather thong to make them spin around and around. Tops can be made from wood or clay.

Hoops

These round toys are made from iron or a thin strip of wood that is bent into a circle. Children run through the streets, pushing the hoops along.

VISIT A SCHOOL

Teachers in Athens will be delighted to show you around their schools. Like all the Greeks, they believe that education is very important because it prepares boys to be good citizens. (Girls do not go to school.) In addition to reading, writing, and mathematics, pupils are taught music, dancing, and sport. The Greeks believe that education should produce "a healthy mind in a healthy body."

Boys from ordinary families finish school when they are about 12 or 13. From then on they are treated as adults. Boys from wealthy families continue their education at advanced levels—they learn about history, science, politics, and philosophy.

Stylus pen

TEACHING GIRLS

Home lessons
Since girls do not go to school, daughters of rich families may have private tutors who teach them to read and write at home.

Useful skills
Most girls learn skills such as spinning, weaving, and housekeeping. Their mothers or senior slaves teach them.

First school
From the age of seven years, boys study with a teacher called a *grammatistes*.

Scholar slave
A slave called a *paedogogus* takes wealthy pupils to and from school and makes sure that they work hard.

Carpenter

Boys from ordinary working families do not spend much time at school. Some do not go at all. Their fathers teach them the skills they will need to earn a living when they are grown up. They learn by watching, helping, and asking lots of questions!

Fisherman

In Athens, all young men from citizen families have to join the army when they are 18. They serve for two years and can be called up to fight any time the city is at war.

Music teacher
Teachers called *citharistes* teach boys how to recite poetry, sing songs, and play the flute and the lyre.

SOCRATES
(Born 469 B.C.)

Socrates is the most famous thinker and teacher in Athens. After an early career in the army, he has devoted the rest of his life to studying. He once studied science, but recently has become more interested in philosophy. He is trying to find out what makes people achieve greatness and what makes cities like Athens so great.

Socrates and pupils

Socrates teaches his students to ask questions about everything. He is sure that is the best way to learn! This makes him very unpopular with the Athens city council—they do not like him asking awkward questions about how the city is run. They fear that Socrates will teach young people to criticize the state and how it is organized.

Sport is an important part of education for Greek boys. A special games teacher, called a paidotribes, takes them to a gymnasium (sports center) or to a palaestra (wrestling ground) to practice their sporting skills.

GOING TO THE THEATER

A day at the theater could prove to be the highlight of your whole visit! Greek theaters are magnificent buildings, and the dramatists—especially in Athens—create extraordinarily powerful plays.

Athenian plays originated around 550 B.C. as songs and dances performed by men at religious festivals in honor of the god Dionysus. Today, actors and choruses perform specially written plays in the huge theater of Dionysus on the lower slopes of the Acropolis. Women are not allowed to act, so men dressed in wigs and women's clothing also play the female parts. There are three main actors, and sometimes junior actors as well. The chorus performs at the front of the stage and comments on events as they happen in the play. This makes the drama even more intense!

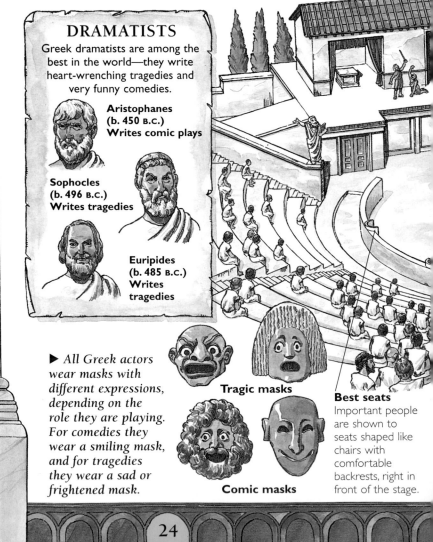

DRAMATISTS

Greek dramatists are among the best in the world—they write heart-wrenching tragedies and very funny comedies.

Aristophanes (b. 450 B.C.) Writes comic plays

Sophocles (b. 496 B.C.) Writes tragedies

Euripides (b. 485 B.C.) Writes tragedies

▶ *All Greek actors wear masks with different expressions, depending on the role they are playing. For comedies they wear a smiling mask, and for tragedies they wear a sad or frightened mask.*

Tragic masks

Comic masks

Best seats
Important people are shown to seats shaped like chairs with comfortable backrests, right in front of the stage.

THEATER DESIGN

Greek theaters are hollowed out of steep hillsides. Their semicircular shape means that sounds made by the actors carry well. Everyone gets a good view of the stage, too.

Proscenium
Skene
Ramp
Ramp
Parados
Parados
Orchestra
Seats

WHO TO LOOK OUT FOR AT THE THEATER

Actors

Energetic, with good memories, they may play several different roles just by changing masks.

Chorus

Very well-trained actors, they sing and dance. For a comedy they wear bright clothes; for a tragedy, they wear dark.

Satyrs

Actors from the chorus dressed as half-man, half-beast. They make fun of tragic plays.

Stagehands

They paint the scenery on the the wall at the back of the stage, called the *skene*

On stage
Actors perform on this raised stage, called the *proscenium*. The chorus performs on the *orchestra*, the circular area in front. Actors wait in side corridors called *paradoi* before going on.

▲ *The audience is mostly men. Athenians think that tragic plays are too upsetting for women to watch, and that comic plays are too vulgar. You will have to pay for your seats—the city only gives free entry tokens to citizens who cannot afford the price.*

June/July

Panathenaia, in
honor of Athena.

Oct/Nov

Processions in
honor of Zeus.

Nov/Dec

Poseidea, in honor
of Poseidon.

Jan/Feb

Anthesteria
(children's
festival).

Feb/March

Festival of
Artemis, goddess
of hunting.

March/April

Dionysia (main
drama festival).

April/May

Washing Athena's
statue ceremony.

May/June

Skira, harvest
festival.

**N.B. The Athenian
year begins in
midsummer**

FESTIVAL TIME

The Athenians organize more than 40 festivals to honor their gods and goddesses. Most are held outside in spring and summer. Athenian festivals are celebrated in many different ways with prayers, sacrifices, processions, music and drama, and athletic games.

All the festivals are ancient but they have many different origins. Some are rituals left over from when Athens was ruled by kings. Others are designed to increase citizens' sense of patriotism and pride. Some mark important stages in people's lives, such as getting married, and others are farming festivals in which the season's crops are blessed.

▶ *The Thesmophoria festival is held in Athens every fall. Preparation for this event begins in the spring. Its purpose is to thank Demeter, the goddess of fertility, for sending food, crops, and healthy children—and to ask her to send more in the future. The details of what happens at this festival are kept secret from the men—it is a strictly women-only event!*

The camp
The women stay in the camp for three days while the men—or their slaves— look after their homes.

Offerings
In spring, women throw piglets and cakes shaped like snakes into holy hollows in the ground as offerings to the goddess Demeter.

Digging up
In fall, at the start of the Thesmophoria festival, the women dig up the offerings they made in spring. The offerings are rotten and very smelly by now!

The altar
The women carry the smelly remains and place them on Demeter's altar. They ask the goddess to bless them and make the crops grow in the fields.

Day of fasting

On the second day of the festival, women eat no solid food and sit on the ground. By performing this ritual, the women believe they are conserving their own energy and transferring their strength to the crops.

Altar

Shelter

THE ATHENIAN CALENDAR

Greeks measure time by observing the moon and the sun, by yearly religious festivals, by the changing seasons, or by counting "Olympiads" (the four-year period between each Olympic games). The Athenians divide the year into 12 months. Each month, measured from new moon to new moon, is 29 or 30 days long.

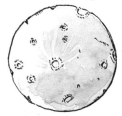

The year, beginning in midsummer, contains 354 days. As it takes the earth 365¼ days to orbit the sun, after a while, the calendar falls out of step with the seasons. To make up the difference, a month is repeated from time to time.

Ritual shouting

On the second night of the festival, the women gather together in the camp and shout insults at one another. This is completely opposite to their normal behavior —a sign that this is a special, holy time.

GETTING THERE

The Thesmophoria festival takes place on open ground just to the south of the Pnyx Hill, where the citizens' Assembly meets. The women gather here on the first day of the festival and set up camp.

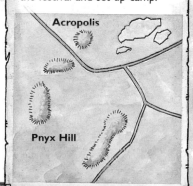

Acropolis

Pnyx Hill

Sowing seeds

Later, the rotten remains are mixed with seeds of grain and scattered on the fields.

Buildings

This circular building is called the Tholos. The Council meets here. Councilors on 24-hour duty sleep here, too.

Officials

These men are appointed by the Council to check prices, weights, and measures. They are also able to arrest thieves.

Statues

Ever since 508 B.C., the citizens of Athens have been organized into ten tribes named after famous heroes. Their statues stand here in the marketplace.

Acrobats

Acrobats and gymnasts travel from city to city putting on shows in the marketplace.

GOING SHOPPING

Athens is one of the richest cities in Greece and, because of its fine harbor at Piraeus, has become a great center of international trade. You can find goods here from countries all around the Mediterranean—but they are expensive!

The best place to shop is in the agora. Its name means "meeting place," and many years ago, the citizens' Assembly met here. But today the agora is the commercial center of Athens. Farmers, fishermen, merchants, and craft workers bring their goods to sell. It is also possible to buy craft goods like pottery directly from workshops nearby. It is very safe to shop here— citizens with criminal records are not allowed to trade in the agora.

▶ *The agora covers a vast area. People selling farm produce or food and drink set up their stalls in the open space in the middle. Merchants selling more expensive goods have shops in the stoas (covered walkways).*

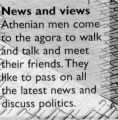

MONEY

In Greece, there are two types of coin—old and new style—that are most commonly used for buying goods. Old-style coins, made mostly before c. 480 B.C., have an owl on them (Athena's symbol). These coins are often called "owls," as a nickname. New-style coins, made mostly after c. 480 B.C., are usually decorated with pictures of gods and heroes.

Stoas

News and views
Athenian men come to the agora to walk and talk and meet their friends. They like to pass on all the latest news and discuss politics.

WHAT YOU CAN BUY AT THE MARKET

Papyrus
This is thick, smooth paper made from reeds. It comes from Egypt.

Olive oil
Made from crushed olives grown on farms near Athens. It is used for cooking, lighting, or beauty care.

Sponges
All around the Greek coast, divers search the sea floor to gather these sponges.

Fabrics
Homespun wool for everyday use and fine linen are both on sale here.

VISIT TO A WORKSHOP

Pottery techniques
Athenian potters work in small potteries, employing just five or six men. Most Athenian pots are thrown on a wheel and expertly decorated by hand. Pots in fashion now are decorated in "red-figure" style: gods and goddesses, heroes, and scenes from everyday life all appear in a warm red color against a shiny black background.

Stamnos   Psykter   Hydria

Lebes   Squat lekythos

Lekythos   Oinochoe

Athenian craftsmen make pots in many different shapes and sizes. Each type of pot has a special purpose and a special name.

On display
Valuable goods, like fine pottery, imported silk cloth, or slaves, are displayed on low stone platforms called *kikloi*.

EATING OUT

The market

You'll find plenty of stalls here that sell snacks. Try bread topped with sesame seeds, dried grapes, and goat's cheese.

Breakfast time

For an early breakfast, many Greeks eat yesterday's bread dipped in a little wine.

At the temple

On festival days, join the crowds outside a big temple. The priests will hand out slices of roast meat—a luxury!

Most Greek people eat at home, but they do entertain with special dinner parties called *symposia*. Once you have made some Greek friends, you will almost certainly be invited to share a meal with them. Don't be surprised if you don't all eat together. Greek families normally entertain their male and female guests in different rooms!

Greek food is simple, but very healthy. It can be strongly flavored—full of onions, garlic, and fresh herbs. Meat may not be on the menu—just lots of bread, oatmeal, fruit, and vegetables, with a little fish or cheese. In winter, you may be offered some warming lentil soup.

Bread and oatmeal
These are essential to a Greek diet. They are made from wheat and oats.

Table talk
Food and drink are arranged on low tables for diners to help themselves.

Men only
Male guests prepare for the *symposion* by putting on clean clothes, scenting their hair, and wearing garlands of flowers.

Wine and water
Wine is always served with dinner. The Greeks drink their wine mixed with water.

Fresh octopus
A real treat! You can find fresh fish and seafood at the agora, but it is very expensive.

Goat's cheese and olives
Favorite Greek food! Eat these with bread, fresh herbs, or vegetables.

Figs and pears
These are a sweet and delicious end to the meal. They ripen well in the summer sun.

Honey cakes
These are made from the valuable honey from Mount Hymettus, close to Athens.

Wine
Made from grapes picked in September. Older wine has the best flavor, but it is strong!

◀ *Greek men and women do not mix at dinner parties. But wealthy women sometimes give private dinners for their female friends. Poor women have more freedom. They are allowed out to meet friends while shopping or to fetch water from the well.*

Entertainers
Hetaira means "companion." It is the name for women who have been trained to entertain with conversation, music, and dancing.

▼ *Male guests are shown into the* andron—*a dining room set apart for men to use after the rest of the family has eaten. The other guests will also be men. The only women present will be the entertainers.*

DO'S AND DON'TS

Do pour an offering of wine to the gods. This shows respect.

Do lie down sideways on your couch to eat, like your host and his other guests.

Don't feel embarrassed if you feel sleepy—just lie back and snooze! It is normal for all the guests and their hosts to have a nap after eating.

Slaves
The slaves carry food to the dining room. They also clear up all the mess after the guests have gone.

DELPHI & THE ORACLE

Greek people worship many different gods. There are gods for warriors, gods for mothers and babies, gods for doctors, gods for craftsmen, and gods for farmers and shepherds. All these gods are worshiped at special sites called shrines. Make time to visit Delphi, where there is a famous shrine to the god Apollo. It is a very holy place, surrounded by beautiful countryside. At many points on your journey, you will be able to glimpse wonderful views across the sea.

The Greeks believe that the gods can help them in their everyday lives, on special occasions, like getting married, or in times of danger, like going to war. They make offerings to the gods, mostly of food and drink, and hope that the gods will assist them in return. Many people visit Delphi to ask the oracle there for wise advice.

▼ *According to ancient legends, Delphi (below) is the* omphalos, *meaning navel, or center of the earth. Spring is the best time for your visit. Then, the mountain slopes will be carpeted with wildflowers.*

The Pythia
This priestess lives in Apollo's temple at Delphi. She breathes in the poisonous smoke from burning leaves.

▶ *It is believed that holy people or places, called oracles, can foretell the future. The Pythia priestess is the most important oracle in Greece. Worshipers bring their problems to her, hoping she will tell them what to do. Often, her answers are not easy to understand, so the priests in Apollo's temple explain what they mean.*

Mount Olympus
According to ancient legend, the gods live on the snowy peaks of Mount Olympus, the highest mountain in Greece.

●Delphi

Athens●

Burning laurel leaves

The Priest
Priests in Apollo's temple listen to the words the Pythia utters while she is dizzy from the laurel-leaf smoke, and report them to worshipers waiting outside.

GREEK GODS

As you travel around, you will see many statues and carvings of Greek gods and goddesses. To help you identify them, here is a list of some of the most important ones, together with their roles.

Zeus—god of lightning

Hera—goddess of women and female animals

Athena—goddess of wisdom

Apollo—god of music

Poseidon—god of earthquakes and the sea

Artemis—goddess of hunting

Hestia—goddess of hearth and home

Hephaestus—god of blacksmiths

Demeter—goddess of farms

Hermes—messenger of the gods

Ares—god of war

Aphrodite—goddess of love

READ ABOUT THE GODS

Greek writers have composed poems and plays about the gods. Among the most famous are Homer (c. 800 B.C.), who wrote stories about the adventures of gods and men, and Pindar (518–438 B.C.), who wrote about heroes as well as gods. Dramatists Aeschylus (c. 525–458 B.C.) and Euripides (c. 485–406 B.C.) wrote plays about love, hate, good, and evil.

A discus is a circular metal plate about 10 in. (25 cm) in diameter. Athletes try to throw it as far as they can.

Long jump

Athletes carry a 2½ lb (1.13 kg) weight in each hand to help them jump farther. They run to the take off mark, swing their arms forward, then jump.

Wrestling

The three types of wrestling are: upright, on-the-ground, and *pancration* or "all-in" wrestling. Referees will stop a contest if one man raises a finger—the sign of surrender.

Javelin

This began as training for war. Athletes threw a long spear almost 6½ ft (1.98 m) long.

OLYMPIA & THE GAMES

The Olympic games is one of the most magnificent sports festivals in the world. It began in 776 B.C., is held every four years, and lasts for five days.

If you want to visit Olympia, be prepared for large crowds. More than 20,000 spectators flock to the games from all over Greece and the colonies. Foreigners are not usually allowed to attend, but you might like to try to make a special arrangement with the priests at Zeus' temple. Like all other Greek sports festivals, the Olympic games began as a religious festival in honor of the gods, so priests are in charge. If you are lucky enough to get in, you will find that a trip to the games is an exciting day out!

Olympia

LOOK OUT FOR

Judges
They keep a look out for cheating and ensure fair play. Bribing a judge is a serious crime.

Priests
They help the athletes make sacrifices to the gods at the start of the games.

Marshals
They use big sticks to keep order among the athletes and the crowd.

Race-in-armor
The athletes all wear helmets and greaves (leg guards) and carry heavy, round shields.

▶ *The hoplitodromos, or race-in-armor, is a good way to train men to be fit for war. This race was one of the last to be added to the Olympic program in 520 B.C. Twenty-five runners take part, and with all that armor, it is a very noisy and exciting event.*

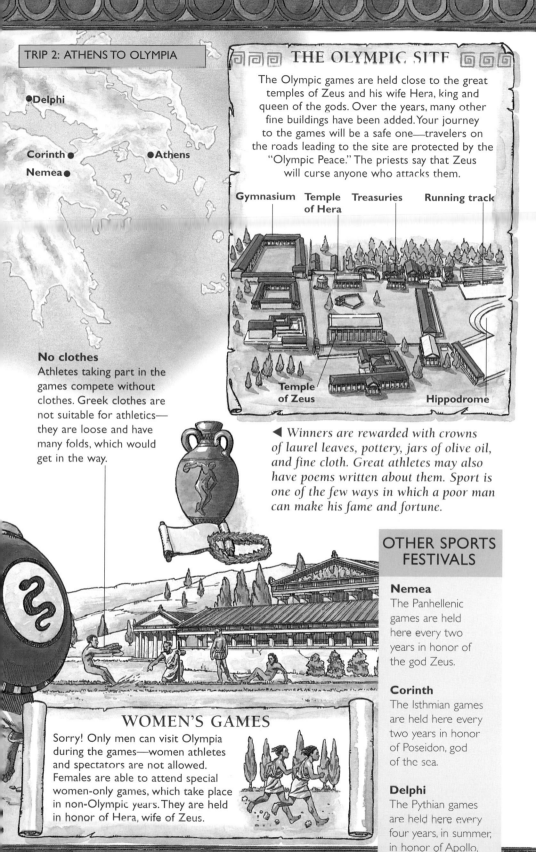

Delphi

Corinth

Nemea

Athens

THE OLYMPIC SITE

The Olympic games are held close to the great temples of Zeus and his wife Hera, king and queen of the gods. Over the years, many other fine buildings have been added. Your journey to the games will be a safe one—travelers on the roads leading to the site are protected by the "Olympic Peace." The priests say that Zeus will curse anyone who attacks them.

Gymnasium Temple of Hera Treasuries Running track

Temple of Zeus Hippodrome

No clothes

Athletes taking part in the games compete without clothes. Greek clothes are not suitable for athletics—they are loose and have many folds, which would get in the way.

◀ Winners are rewarded with crowns of laurel leaves, pottery, jars of olive oil, and fine cloth. Great athletes may also have poems written about them. Sport is one of the few ways in which a poor man can make his fame and fortune.

OTHER SPORTS FESTIVALS

Nemea
The Panhellenic games are held here every two years in honor of the god Zeus.

Corinth
The Isthmian games are held here every two years in honor of Poseidon, god of the sea.

Delphi
The Pythian games are held here every four years, in summer, in honor of Apollo, god of music and philosophy.

WOMEN'S GAMES

Sorry! Only men can visit Olympia during the games—women athletes and spectators are not allowed. Females are able to attend special women-only games, which take place in non-Olympic years. They are held in honor of Hera, wife of Zeus.

35

Government officials examine all newborn babies and reject weak, sickly ones. They are left to die on a mountainside.

Leaving home

Boys are taken away from home when they are seven years old and sent to live in army barracks. They are brought up by teachers.

Toughness

Spartan boys are beaten and half-starved to teach them toughness. Some of them die.

The army

Spartan teachers aim to turn boys into strong, fearless warriors. All Spartan boys from citizen families have to join the army when they grow up.

SPARTA

You may find it difficult to get permission to visit this rugged city-state in the southern Peloponnese region. Foreigners are not normally allowed in, but keep trying! Sparta is a fascinating place, and well worth exploring.

Sparta was once a rich city, with skilled craft workers and merchants who imported luxury goods from abroad. After many attacks from nearby cities, the government decided they had to do more to protect its people. So they completely reorganized city life. Now, all citizens devote their lives to war. Two other groups of people live in Sparta: the *perioikoi*, who work as traders, and the *helots*, slaves who farm the land.

Army life
Soldiers live in barracks, where conditions are grim. The beds are made of straw and the food is horrible.

Long hair
Unlike other Greek men, Spartan soldiers grow their hair long. They comb it and arrange it over their shoulders before going into battle.

DO'S AND DON'TS

✓ Make an offering to the goddess Artemis. You can buy a little statue—the usual offering—from the priests here.

✗ Don't talk to *helots*, or try to make friends with them—the Spartans will think you are encouraging them to revolt!

Helots
Each Spartan soldier is given land by the state, plus *helots* (slaves) to farm it. The *helots* grow food to feed soldiers and their families.

SPARTAN WOMEN

Spartan girls

Spartan girls live at home with their mothers. They are taught gymnastics, dancing, and many sports. They must be very obedient.

Spartan women

Spartan women are made to take exercise so that they will produce strong, healthy babies. They spend very little time with their husbands or sons, who live in army barracks.

A history of conflict

Athens is one of Sparta's fiercest enemies. They have been at war since 431 B.C. Argos is another of Sparta's enemies. Athens and Argos often join together to attack Spartan lands. But the Spartan citizens and rulers fear another enemy even more. They are frightened that their *helots* will rebel. They did this once before, in 630 B.C. That is why all Spartan men are soldiers, ready to defend their city-state from *helot* attack.

► *Sparta's system of government is very different from that in the other city-states—only a few people are allowed to make the decisions.*

Two kings
Lead the army in war.

Five *Ephors* (overseers)
Officials chosen by the Assembly to supervise government business.

The *Gerousia* (council)
Plan government policy, are judges, and pass new laws. Made up of 28 councilors, all over 60, plus two kings.

The *Apella* (Assembly)
All citizens over 30. Votes (by shouting) to accept or reject government plans.

SPARTAN GOVERNMENT

VISIT TO THE NEW PORTS

One of Athens' top generals during the Persian Wars. He also organized the building of the famous long walls, linking Athens to Piraeus and the new navy harbors.

A thens has two new harbors, at Zea and Munychia, specially built to shelter its new warships. The biggest, Zea, has huge stone boat sheds and dry docks, where repairs are carried out. Athens is famous for having the strongest navy in all Greece—it is a sight not to be missed!

The harbors, which are close to the busy trading port of Piraeus, are fascinating places to visit. With luck, you may be able to climb inside one of the huge warships! The harbors are an easy day trip from Athens and all along the way you'll be perfectly safe. The whole route is well protected by strong stone walls, built in 479–478 B.C., and extended in 458 B.C.

Linen sails

Xerxes I, King of Persia (ruled 486–466 B.C.)

Xerxes means "ruler of heroes." He is famous for leading a mighty army to invade Greece in 480 B.C. However, they were defeated at the Battle of Plataea in 479 B.C.

▶ *In 490 B.C., General Themistocles persuaded the Athenian citizens to build a new fleet of warships to help defend Greece. The money to pay for them came from silver mines at Laurium. The biggest Greek warships are called* triremes—*they are about 135 ft (41 m) long and 20 ft (6 m) wide. They are able to reach speeds of 10 miles (16 km) per hour. Athens has over 200 of them—all magnificent!*

Prow

Bronze spike

Sea-battle tactics
Ships try to smash and sink one another using sharp metal-tipped rams fitted to their prows. If this fails, they then sail close together until they are side by side. Soldiers leap from deck to deck, killing their enemies and trying to force them overboard.

Lysander, Spartan admiral

Look out for this up-and-coming Spartan soldier. He is already making a name for himself in the Peloponnesian War against Athens, which began in 431 B.C. Military experts predict a splendid career for him.

◀ **The Battle of Salamis** marked one of the turning points in the Persian Wars. It took place in 480 B.C., close to the little island of Salamis, just off the coast near Athens. The Persians were defeated after General Themistocles lured their fleet into the narrow strip of water between Salamis and the mainland. There they were attacked and sunk by the Athenian fleet that was lying in wait.

AEGEAN SEA

Plataea ●

● Marathon

Piraeus ● ● Athens

Salamis

Oars

Steering oars

HOPLITE SOLDIERS

Long bronze-tipped spear

Helmet (Athenian style)

Shield (with city or family crest)

Cuirass (breastplate made of bronze, leather, or linen)

Tunic

Greaves (leg guards— bronze or leather)

Long sword with iron blade

Most Greek men fight as foot soldiers known as *hoplites*. *Hoplon* is the Greek word for shield. In battle, the men advance side by side in *phalanx* formation (*see below*), presenting a wall of spears to their enemy. Each man has to buy his own armor and weapons. Men from poor families, who cannot afford to buy weapons, fight with slingshots or bows and arrows, and wear thick fur or leather cloaks instead of armor. Men from rich families, who can afford to buy and feed horses, serve in the cavalry.

Phalanx

Warship crews

Each ship has a crew of around 200 men— 170 to row it, plus another 30 to command it, steer it, keep lookout, and handle the sails. The rowers sit in three rows, on either side of the ship.

THE BATTLE OF MARATHON

Another famous victory for the Greeks happened in 490 B.C. at the Battle of Marathon. The Persians were defeated by a highly trained army of foot soldiers. If you are interested in seeing the Marathon battlefield, an excursion can easily be arranged—Marathon is just 26 miles (42 km) away from Athens' city center.

Burial mound for dead Athenian soldiers at Marathon

The best pottery is made in Athens and Corinth, but you should be able to find interesting examples of local styles on many islands. Some of the best perfume in the whole of Greece is made on the island of Rhodes.

Produce

Fish and all kinds of seafood, such as squid, octopus, mussels, sea urchins, and prawns can be bought from local fisherman down by the harbor. On some islands you can also buy sea produce such as corals and shells.

ISLAND VISITS

As you will have discovered on your journeys through Greece, nowhere on the mainland is very far from the coast. But islanders live closer to the sea than other Greeks. They have to learn to cope with the changeable island weather that sometimes prevents travel. Many island families depend on the sea for their living. Men work as fishermen, sailors, and boatbuilders, while women spin twine for fishing nets and preserve any surplus fish by salting and drying.

Although Greek island scenery is beautiful, life on some islands is hard. The soil is stony and fresh water scarce. Because of this, many islanders have founded Greek colonies on the shores of the Mediterranean where there is more fertile land.

▼ *There are islands all around the Greek coast. Some are big, others are small, some are covered in trees, and others are rocky and barren. Island people have their own special, local customs and traditions.*

Ithaca ——

Zacynthus

IONIAN SEA

Ithaca
This island is the home of Odysseus, hero of the poem, the *Odyssey*, by Homer. Odysseus' wife, Penelope, waited patiently on Ithaca for 10 years for his return from adventures at sea.

Grape vines
Farmers plant vines on wooden poles outside their houses. In fall, they crush the grapes with their feet and make wine with the juice.

Goats
Goats roam across the islands, eating shrubs and wild herbs that grow there. Young boys look after them.

Harbor

40

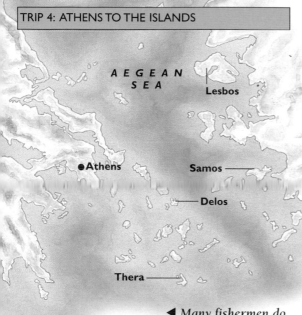

AEGEAN SEA

Lesbos

Athens

Samos

Delos

Thera

Lesbos

A famous center for the arts—especially music and literature. Sappho, Greece's best-known female poet, lived on Lesbos.

◀ *The sea between Greece and Asia Minor is named after Aegeus, a legendary king of Athens. It is over 250 miles (400 km) at its widest point. Hundreds of islands are scattered across it. People live on almost all of them.*

Protective eye

Family farm

You will see many homes like this as you travel around the islands. They are made of sun-dried earth bricks on a wooden frame. They have clay roof tiles.

◀ *Many fishermen do not like to sail out of sight of land. So book your passage with a skipper who is used to long trips. Make sure there is an eye painted on the bow to keep you safe from the "evil eye" (hate and envy) and turn away bad luck.*

Storeroom

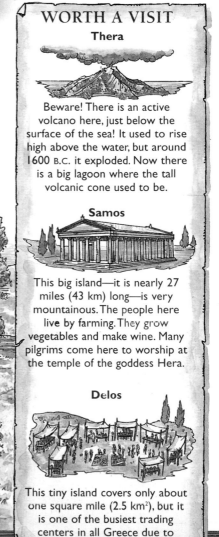

WORTH A VISIT

Thera

Beware! There is an active volcano here, just below the surface of the sea! It used to rise high above the water, but around 1600 B.C. it exploded. Now there is a big lagoon where the tall volcanic cone used to be.

Samos

This big island—it is nearly 27 miles (43 km) long—is very mountainous. The people here live by farming. They grow vegetables and make wine. Many pilgrims come here to worship at the temple of the goddess Hera.

Delos

This tiny island covers only about one square mile (2.5 km²), but it is one of the busiest trading centers in all Greece due to its central location.

LANGUAGE

The Greeks think their language is the best in the world. It is very precise—which makes it especially suitable for scientists and philosophers—and sounds very beautiful, too. The Greeks call foreigners "barbarians," because they do not speak Greek, but instead make ugly noises, sounding like "bar-bar-bar!" The Greek language is many hundreds of years old, but the present-day Greek alphabet was only developed about 800 B.C. It is based on a system of writing invented by the Phoenicians, but with many additions and improvements. Most Greek citizens use this alphabet, with minor variations, but people also use local dialect words, and speak with regional accents. Scholars and artists working in different city-states also write or carve letters in different local styles.

The inscription on this discus reads "Simos made me."

THE GREEK ALPHABET

Name			Sounds
alpha	A	α	a
beta	B	β	b
gamma	Γ	γ	g
delta	Δ	δ	d
epsilon	E	ε	e
zeta	Z	ζ	zd
eta	H	η	e
theta	Θ	θ	th
iota	I	ι	i
kappa	K	κ	k
lambda	Λ	λ	l
mu	M	μ	m
nu	N	ν	n
xi	Ξ	ξ	ks
omicron	O	ο	o
pi	Π	π	p
rho	P	ρ	r
sigma	Σ	σ	s
tau	T	τ	t
upsilon	Y	υ	u
phi	Φ	φ	f/ph
chi	X	χ	kh
psi	Ψ	ψ	ps
omega	Ω	ω	o

USEFUL PHRASES

Pronounce these words as English, but stress the vowels in **bold** type and remember: Greek **ai** sounds like **i** in kite; **ei** as in p**e**t (even at the end of a word); **o**, **i**, **a** as in p**o**t, p**i**t, p**a**t; **ē** like the word **air** and **ou** as in y**ou**. We have added a rough guide in ordinary spelling to help you pronounce each phrase. Please note that the Greeks use the same word for "hello" and "goodbye!"

HELLO/GOODBYE
khaire (say **khy**-re)

PLEASE
ei soi dok**ei** (say ay soy dok-**ay**)

THANK YOU
kh**a**rin **oi**da soi (say **khar**-in **oy**-da soy)

PLEASE CAN I STAY HERE?
ex-esti moi enth**a**de m**e**nein? (say **ex**-ess-ti moy en-**tha**-de **men**-ayn)

YES, YOU CAN
nai, **ex**esti (say ny, **ex**-ess-ti)

NO, YOU CAN'T
ouk **ex**esti (say ook **ex**-ess-ti)

HOW MUCH?
p**o**son? (say **poss**-on)

I DON'T KNOW WHERE I AM
ouk **oi**da hopou eim**i** (say ook **oy**-da **hop**-oo ay-**mi**)

HELP!
bo**ē**thei! (say bo-**air**-thay)

MONEY

Until around 600 B.C., Greek people did not use coins. Instead, they traded by barter—exchanging the goods they had for goods of the same value they wanted. This could be a slow, awkward way to do business, so, when the Greeks heard that Lydian craftworkers had invented coins, they hurried to copy them. In the 5th century B.C., almost all traders prefer to buy and sell using coins. The Greeks have three units of money—obols, drachmas, and staters. Citizens in Athens earn about three obols for a day's work.

Greek coins are made of silver or gold. Each city-state issues its own in all different sizes. For example, a drachma from Athens weighs about 0.15 oz (4.25 g), but a drachma from Aegina weighs about 0.2 oz (5.6 g). Traders in each city only accept their own local coins. So, as you travel around Greece, you will need many different kinds of coins to buy food and drink, to pay for transportation and lodging, and to purchase souvenirs. This need not be a problem. You will find money changers in most big towns. They usually set up their stalls in the market square. They will weigh the "foreign" coins you give them using a balance and give you local ones in return. All money changers charge a fee for their services. Some have become so rich this way that they act as bankers, too. They lend money and provide safe storage for coins and valuable goods.

MOST COMMON COINS

Half obol

Obol

Triobol (3 obols)

Didrachm (two drachmas)

Hemiobol (half obol)

Tetradrachm (four drachmas)

Drachma

Decadrachm (ten drachmas)

Stater

WEIGHTS AND MEASURES

Greeks measure dry weight in units called *talents* and liquids in units called *metretes*. One talent equals 56.9 lb (25.80 kg) and a *metrete* equals 10.4 gallons (47.2 l). Greeks measure length and distance in units based on the human body—the finger measuring 0.75 in. (1.9 cm) and the foot measuring 12.2 in. (31 cm).

24 fingers = 1 Olympic cubit, 18.2 inches (46 cm)

16 fingers = 1 (Greek) foot

600 (Greek) feet = 1 stadion, 584 feet (178 m)

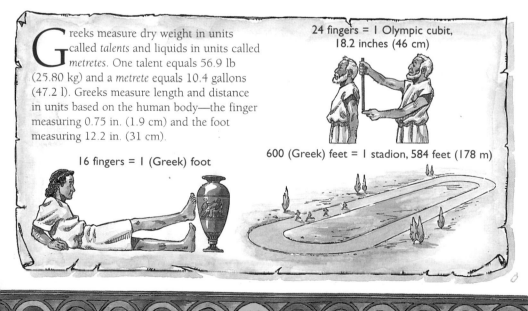

MEDICINE

If you fall ill during your visit—don't worry! There are many excellent doctors in Greece. They can treat you in two different ways. Traditional doctors believe that illness is a punishment sent by the gods, and that saying prayers or offering sacrifices is the best way to seek a cure. Modern doctors have a more scientific approach. They will ask you careful questions about your eating habits, lifestyle,

environment, and state of mind to try to discover what has caused your disease. As a cure, they will prescribe special foods, exercises, or medicines made from herbs. They might also suggest that you sleep overnight in a temple dedicated to the god Asclepius, in the hope that he will send you a message in your dreams, telling you how to get better.

SHRINES

As you explore Athens, you will see shrines dedicated to Asclepius, god of medicine. These are all newly built—the worship of Asclepius has just spread to Athens from its main center at Epidaurus in southern Greece. If you visit during the months of *Boedromion* (Aug–Sept) or *Elaphebolion* (Feb–Mar), you may be able to see—or even take part in—two new festivals in honor of Asclepius, called the *Epidauria* and the *Aesclepia*.

Thanks offerings
Grateful patients who have been cured by Asclepius often have models made of the part of their body he has healed. They leave these models in his temples, to show how thankful they are.

SCIENTISTS AND MATHEMATICIANS

Anaximander (c. 610–545 B.C.) Geographer and astronomer. He believed that the earth is at the center of the universe and drew the first Greek world map.

Anaxagoras (c. 500 B.C. –428 B.C.) A well-known scientist. In his book *On Nature*, he explains his theories about how the universe works. He found out what causes eclipses of the moon.

Hippodamus (around 5th century B.C.) Mathematician, architect, and planner. He rebuilt many important Greek towns, including Piraeus, port of Athens, using gridlike layouts.

MATH AND SCIENCE

In the past, Greek people used myths and legends to explain how the world worked. But today, Greek scholars have a much more scientific approach. They observe and investigate the world around them to try and answer important questions like, "What is matter made of?," "Is the earth the center of the universe?," "Why does the moon shine?," and "How did life begin?" Greek mathematicians have discovered many important laws about how numbers work. They also study the best way to measure things. Their information has proved very useful to architects and builders and to sailors. If you'd like to visit a famous scientist or mathematician, just ask. There are many working and teaching in Athens.

SIMPLE SUMS

Using letters for numbers makes day-to-day sums very difficult, so most people use pebbles, their fingers, or an abacus (counting frame) instead. For surveying and marking out foundations, Greek architects and builders use ropes and measuring rods, after doing careful calculations first!

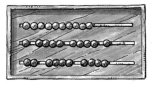

Beads on the top row show numbers 1 to 10
Beads on the middle row show numbers 10 to 100
Beads on the bottom row show numbers 100 to 1,000
All the beads added together = 1,110

You can add or subtract by moving the beads. For example:

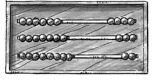

add 200 plus 30 plus 4 = 234

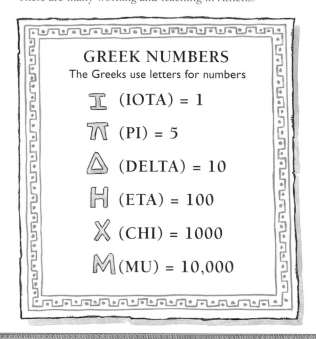

GREEK NUMBERS
The Greeks use letters for numbers

$\mathbb{I}$ (IOTA) = 1

π (PI) = 5

$\triangle$ (DELTA) = 10

H (ETA) = 100

X (CHI) = 1000

M (MU) = 10,000

Pythagoras (c. 580–500 B.C.)
One of the greatest mathematicians who has ever lived! An expert in geometry, he discovered several important mathematical laws. He also started a new religion based on respect for numbers.

Hippocrates (born 460 B.C.)
Doctor, famous throughout Greece. He runs the best medical training school, and has drawn up a code of conduct, called the "Hippocratic Oath," a national standard of good practice for doctors.

Thales of Miletus (c. 636–546 B.C.)
By profession an army engineer. He also traveled to Egypt to measure the pyramids, to study astronomy, and investigate the origins of life on earth.

PRONUNCIATION OF GREEK WORDS

Aeschylus—EESK-ee-lus
Alcibiades—Al-SIB-ay-ah-deez
Anaxagoras—An-axe-AG-or-ass
Aphrodite—Aff-ro-DYE-tee
Apollo—APP-oll-oh
Ares—AIR-eez
Aristophanes—Aris-TOFF-an-eez
Artemis—Ar-TEE-miss
Asclepius—Ask-LEAP-ee-uss
Aspasia—Ass-PAZE-ee-ah

Athena—Ath-EE-nah
Cleisthenes—KLYS-then-eez
Demeter—DEM-ett-er
Dionysos—Dye-on-EYE-sos
Erechtheus—Ere-eck-THEE-us
Hephaestos—Heph-EES-tos
Hera—HERE-ah
Hermes—HER-meez
Hestia—HESS-tee-yah
Hippocrates—Hipp-OCK-rah-teez

Peisistratos—Pie-SIS-tra-toss
Pericles—Per-ICK-leez
Poseidon—Poz-EYE-don
Pythagoras—Py-THAG-or-ass
Sophocles—SOPH-ock-leez
Thales—THAY-leez
Themistocles—Them-ISS-toe-cleez
Thucydides—Thew-SID-id-eez
Xerxes—ZERK-zeez
Zeus—ZEE-yous